Chec
The Success

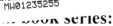
... ~~~~ series:

Also by Honorée Corder:

If Divorce is a Game, These are the Rules: 8 Rules for Thriving Before, During & After Divorce

Vision to Reality: How Short Term Massive Action Equals Long Term Maximum Results

Tall Order! 7 Master Strategies to Organize Your Life and Double Your Success in Half the Time

Play2Pay: How to Market Your College-Bound Student-Athlete for Scholarship Money

Paying4College: How to Save 25-50% on Your Child's College Education

The Successful Single Mom *Cooks!* Cookbook
7 Ingredients or Less - On Your Table in 20 Minutes

Honorée Corder & Grace Bascos

Published by Honorée Enterprises Publishing, LLC

ISBN 978-0-9916-6961-5

Discover other titles by Honorée Corder at
http://www.HonoreeCorder.com,
and everywhere books are sold.

TABLE OF CONTENTS

Dear Reader,

Single moms have so much to do! Raise the kids, go to work, do the laundry, help with homework … and cook dinner? For all of my years as a single mom, I felt like a failure in the "cooking healthy meals" category. I really wanted to make a balanced breakfast to give my daughter a great start to the day, pack her lunch with multiple creative Martha Stewart-esque yummies, cook a healthy dinner every night, yet I found myself downing a protein shake while I made yet another PB&J sandwich or pot of beans and wieners.

By the time I got home, I was exhausted! I had been up since 5 a.m., run a million miles an hour for over twelve hours and when I got home, all I wanted to do was just sit down, watch TV and fall asleep. And … my kid was still hungry!

What to do? I went in search of healthy, home-cooked meals that contained a manageable number of ingredients and would be ready and on the table in about 20 minutes.

What I discovered was that there were so many healthy and nutritious recipes I could make that my daughter would actually eat! Not only that, she would ask for them over and over!

I knew if I was experiencing this challenge, other single moms were, too. While I really compiled this cookbook for me as a reference and reminder, I knew my fellow single moms would benefit from it, too.

I reached out to Grace, my co-writer, because I'm not a cook, chef or self-proclaimed foodie … and she is all of these things. Together we have created this cookbook with the intention of helping single moms everywhere feed their kids easily, simply and deliciously!

We hope you and your kids enjoy these recipes, and are inspired to cook and eat together often.

To Your Health, Happiness & Success,

Honorée & Grace

Tips for the Single Mom Cook

In case you're a novice (like Honorée), here are some helpful tips to get you started.

Think ahead.

You know that dinner is needed, well, pretty much every night. Sundays are a good day to look at your and your kids' schedules, figure out what days are going to be more jam-packed than others, and plan accordingly. Try to plan a tentative nightly menu and stick to as much as possible (we know, just because you write down "tuna melts" for Wednesday doesn't mean you'll have a taste for it that night), and stick it on the fridge. Glance at the list the night before or in the morning to see if you have to take anything out to defrost, or if you need to stop by the store on the way home to pick something up. Sunday is also a great day to make a big meal of a dish that can last throughout the week that can be warmed up in a pinch when there's no time/energy left to get dinner on the table.

Which leads us to: Leftovers are your friend!

There's bound to be a night where you have to succumb to take out for dinner. Opt for healthy, balanced dishes, rather than something calorically empty like pizza or fried chicken or fast food. These are foods that are likely to be eaten all in one sitting, are high in fat and low in nutrition. For example, Asian leftovers can be reheated easily, and made into a brand new stir-fry with the addition of frozen vegetables and leftover rice is transformed into fried rice (extra points for ordering brown rice instead of steamed rice!). Always be thinking of ways you can incorporate/transform leftovers into something for the next night

Shop smart.

On your big grocery shopping days, always make sure you have the staples on hand: whole wheat pastas, tortillas (can be frozen separately and thawed when needed), cans of whole peeled tomatoes, frozen vegetables that can go into anything, such as peas, carrots, pearl onions, and corn. If you buy larger packages of chicken or other meats, separate and freeze them into manageable portions when you get home.

Don't be afraid of day-of grocery shopping.

We know, ten minutes in a grocery store can seem like an hour, but stopping in to get a few fresh ingredients will give your meal that more home-cooked feel and flavor. I like to buy bunches of green onions to chop and use as garnish on a lot of my dishes, and its flavor goes a long way! Have a hankering for a dish that night? Write a very specific grocery list of things you need for the meal, go to the store and STICK TO THE LIST. Plus, if you've completely forgotten to take that frozen chicken or beef out of the freezer, those items are there, ready and waiting to be taken home and cooked.

Kids can cook, too!

They might not be ready to wield a knife, but they can stir pots, or rinse and strain vegetables. Getting them involved also takes a bit of pressure off of you to get everything done, and it turns what can sometimes seem like a task into quality time spent together. The sooner you get them to help you with the small tasks, the more useful... er, we mean, interested they will become in cooking as they get older.

A well-rounded meal.

We won't get into the whole carb vs. no carb argument but growing kids need a well-balanced diet. And that includes proteins, vegetables AND carbohydrates. Incorporating these three elements into every tasty meal at home means they won't be scared by vegetables out at restaurants or at other kids' houses (where you hope and pray they are serving vegetables as well!).

Make it your own.

Following a recipe to a "T" ensures that the dish will taste the way the recipe-writer intended. But that doesn't mean YOU may like it that exact way. Think the dish could benefit from a little garlic? Add some chopped garlic at the beginning or garlic powder at the end. Not into spice? Omit the jalapeno peppers or chili powder, but make sure you compensate for flavor with a favorite spice or herbs of your own. Add in extra vegetables to make amp up the nutritional value. Unless the recipe writer is sitting down with you to dinner, this is your meal, make it how you want.

Make sure it tastes good.

Yes, we all want to sit down to a quick and healthy meal, but it's all for naught if it doesn't make you and the kids say "mmmmmm!" Taste the dish throughout the cooking process, after you've added some seasoning or spices, make sure it's to your liking. Make it something that you want to eat again and again, and a favorite on your child's dinner roster. You have to eat every day, you might as well enjoy it, right?

Recipes for Everyone

Turkey Burgers

A turkey burger with flavor, yet they are not overly spicy or hot!!

Ingredients

1 lb. ground turkey
1 egg, beaten
1 tbsp. Worcestershire sauce
½ tsp. salt
½ tsp. garlic powder
½ tsp. onion powder
½ cup seasoned dry breadcrumbs

Directions

1. Mix all of the ingredients together and form into 6 patties.

2. Grill until the centers of the burgers are no longer pink.

3. You could also do these on the stove or even in the oven. Just make sure to use a meat thermometer or make sure the center is not pink.

Number of Servings: 6

Tortilla Pizza

A delicious, quick and easy pizza your kids will want to help make and love to eat!

Ingredients

1 whole wheat tortilla
2 Tbs. pizza or tomato sauce
8-10 pepperoni or turkey pepperoni slices
2 Tbs. miscellaneous veggies: green pepper, mushrooms, onions, cauliflower, broccoli
Mozzarella or Cheddar Cheese ~ sprinkle as desired

Directions

1. Pre-heat oven to 350°. Spread sauce to the edges of tortilla. Add pepperoni and veggies. Cover with cheese as desired. Bake for 10-15 minutes, until cheese is melted and tortilla is crisp.

Number of Servings: 1

Taco Soup ~ Chili

Moms can fry up ground beef ahead of time and have their kids pour everything in about 15-20 minutes before she gets home and everyone can sit down and enjoy a hot meal. ~Contributed by Valerie Kleinman

Ingredients

1 lb. ground beef
1 15 oz. can each: Pinto and Kidney Beans
1 28 oz. can Petite Diced Tomatoes
1 15 oz. can of corn
McCormick Original Taco Seasoning Mix*
Hidden Valley Ranch Salad Dressing Mix*

Directions

1. Brown and drain ground beef.

2. Add beans and tomatoes, including liquid, to beef. Bring to boil.

3. Drain corn and add to mixture.

4. Add taco seasoning and ranch dressing mix.

5. Simmer for 15 minutes. Top with any or all of these: sour cream, shredded cheese, green onions, corn chips (Frito Scoops are also good, too!).

6. Serve and enjoy!

Number of Servings: 4

Cook's Note: *It's your best idea to use these brands ... others have been tried and it just didn't turn out as good!

Balsamic Asparagus and Cherry Tomato Salad

I made this tonight and it was super yummy! Even the kids gobbled up and raved about the asparagus!! Shocked!
~Contributed by April Gremillion

Ingredients

1 1/2 pounds asparagus (about 40 spears)
1 cup cherry tomatoes, about 10 cut in half
1 tbsp balsamic vinegar
2 tsp orange juice
1 tsp minced garlic
2 tbsp shredded Parmesan Cheese
Salt and Pepper to taste

Directions

1. Chop woody ends off asparagus. Microwave for 2 to 3 minutes or cook in boiling salted water for about 4 to 6 minutes.

2. Plunge into ice water to stop cooking. Drain.

3. Add cherry tomatoes.

4. Stir together vinegar, orange juice and garlic, season to taste. Spoon dressing over asparagus and tomatoes.

5. Sprinkle with parmesan cheese.

Number of Servings: 4

California Club Wrap

I had these last night for dinner and they were easy and delicious! ~Contributed by April Gremillion

Ingredients

1 medium tortilla, fat-free
2 tbsp store-bought hummus
1 small tomato, thinly sliced
1/4 s small cucumber, thinly sliced
1/2 cup watercress, thick stems discarded**
Salt and Pepper to taste

Directions

1. Lay tortilla on a flat surface and spread with hummus.

2. Layer with tomatoes, cucumber and watercress.

3. Add any veggies you have on hand.

4. Season to taste, roll up tightly and enjoy!

Number of Servings: 1

**I used Romain Lettuce instead of the watercress.

Mexican-Style Chicken-Filled Tortillas

Quick, easy & flavorful ~ a favorite of kids and adults alike.

Ingredients

4 boneless, skinless chicken breast halves, cut into thin bite-sized strips
1 cup frozen whole kernel sweet corn
1 cup chunky-style salsa
1 (2 ¼-oz.) can sliced ripe olives, well drained
8 8-10-inch fat-free whole wheat tortillas
Mozzarella or Cheddar Cheese ~ sprinkle as desired

Directions

1. Spray large nonstick skillet with nonstick cooking spray. Heat over medium-high heat until hot. Add chicken; cook and stir 5 to 6 minutes or until no longer pink.

2. Stir in corn, salsa and olives. Reduce heat to medium; cook 4-6 minutes or until thoroughly heated.

3. Meanwhile, warm tortillas as directed on package. Spoon ¼ of chicken mixture onto half of each tortilla. Fold tortillas over. If desired, serve with lights sour cream and additional salsa.

Number of Servings: 4

Creamy Parmesan Broiled Tilapia

Much to my surprise, my 9-year-old ate this fish! And loved it!

Ingredients

2 Tilapia Fillets (5oz to 6oz each - if frozen, be sure to thaw fully before cooking)
2 teaspoons Light Mayonnaise
2 teaspoons Non-Fat Plain Yogurt
4 Tablespoons Shredded Parmesan Cheese
2 to 4 sprigs of fresh Dill
1 tsp Garlic Powder or Garlic Salt, divided
Black Pepper (use as much or as little as you like)

Directions

1. Place mayonnaise, yogurt and parmesan cheese in a small bowl, mix with a spoon until well combined.

2. Cover a cookie sheet with aluminum and spray with non-stick cooking spray.

3. Set oven to broil on HIGH.

4. Place tilapia fillets onto cookie sheet, about 2 inches apart.

5. Divide the cheese mixture and spread half onto each fillet with a spoon, using the back of the spoon to distribute evenly over fish.

6. Rub dill between your fingers to separate and sprinkle 1 to 2 sprigs worth of leaves over each fillet.

7. Sprinkle each fillet with half of the garlic powder or garlic Salt and desired amount of Black Pepper.

8. Place cookie sheet into oven about 6" below the broiler.

9. Watch fish carefully. Depending on the weight of the fillets it will take between 5-7 minutes to cook fully. When you notice the cheese starting to brown, check fish every 30 seconds to see if it's done. Fish will flake easily with a fork when fully cooked.

10. Turn broiler off and leave fish in oven about 5 minutes. (this is optional, but will ensure it's cooked all the way and give you a chance to finish the rest of your preparation)

11. Remove from oven and serve with side dishes of your choice.

Number of Servings: 2

Turkey and Pepper Pasta

You could use penne, elbow noodles or "squiggly" pasta.

Ingredients

8 oz. (about 2 ½ cups) uncooked pasta
1 16 oz. pkg. frozen mixed (green, red, and yellow) bell pepper*
1 ½ cups cubed cooked turkey
½ cup light soy or skim milk
1 10 ¾ oz. can condensed 98% fat-free cream of chicken soup

Directions

1. Cook pasta to desired firmness, following package directions.

2. While pasta cooks, spray large nonstick skillet with non-stick spray. Heat over medium heat until hot. Add bell peppers and stir-fry about 4-5 minutes until crisp-tender.

3. Add in turkey, milk and soup. Mix well. Cook until hot, about 5 minutes. Add salt and pepper to taste.

4. Mix with pasta and serve.

Number of Servings: 4

Strawberry-Orange Chicken Salad

A salad your kids will eat and love.

Ingredients

Dressing
1 Tbs. red wine vinegar
¼ cup strawberry syrup
Salad
2 cups torn lettuce
2 cups from prewashed fresh spinach
(substitution: 4 cups prepackaged mixed salad greens)
¾ cup sliced cooked chicken, cut into strips
2/3 cup sliced and halved fresh strawberries
1 seedless orange, peeled, cut up

Directions

1. In a small bowl, combine dressing ingredients; mix well.

2. In medium bowl, combine all salad ingredients; toss well. Spoon salad onto 2 individual plates. Drizzle with dressing.

Number of Servings: 2

Sesame Chicken Nuggets

All kids love chicken nuggets, especially when they're a little sweet.

Ingredients

2 tbsp sesame seeds
1 lb. precut chicken breast chunks, or 4 boneless, skinless chicken breast halves, cut into 1-inch chunks
1 tbsp oil
¾ cup barbecue sauce or ½ cup honey

Directions

1. In a large non-stick skillet, over medium heat, toast sesame seeds until golden brown, stirring frequently. Sprinkle toasted seed over chicken chunks.

2. Heat oil in same skillet over medium-high heat until hot. Add chicken; cook and stir 5 to 6 minutes or until chicken is no longer pink. Serve chicken nuggets with sauce.

Number of Servings: 4

Tuna Casserole

I can make this in about 8 minutes!

Ingredients

1 bag egg noodles
1 small can tuna in water
1 cup frozen peas
1 can low-fat Campbell's Mushroom Soup
Salt & pepper to taste

Directions

1. Cook noodles according to directions. Drain and put in medium bowl.

2. Add other ingredients, stir.

3. Microwave for 2 minutes.

4. Serve & eat!

Number of Servings: 2-4

Fried Rice with or without Meat

This recipe is yummy and you can use beef, chicken or shrimp … or go vegetarian!

Ingredients

1 lb. boneless, skinless chicken breast or 18-20 medium shrimp or 1 lb. sliced beef
1 tbsp canola oil
2 cups quick-cook brown or white rice, uncooked
2 cups peas and carrots, frozen
2 cups water
2 tbsp soy sauce
1-2 cups cooked scrambled egg, unseasoned

Directions

1. Cut chicken or beef into bite size cubes and add to oil in skillet, cook through and brown. For shrimp, add to skillet with 2 tbsp water and cook through.

2. Add water, rice, soy sauce, and peas and carrots.

3. Bring to a boil, lower heat and simmer 5-7 minutes covered until liquid is absorbed, stirring frequently.

4. Stir in scrambled eggs and soy sauce to taste.

Number of Servings: 4

Ridiculously Yummy Turkey Burritos

Honorée falls in love immediately with any recipe containing sour cream and cheese. Hopefully you and your kids do, too!

Ingredients

1 ½ cups chopped cooked turkey
1 cup nonfat sour cream
2 tbsp taco seasoning mix
2 oz. 2% shredded cheddar cheese
4 8-inch fat-free flour tortillas

Directions

1. In medium bowl, combine turkey, sour cream, taco seasoning mix and ¼ cup of cheese; mix well.

2. Spread ¼ of mixture down the center of each tortilla; roll up. Sprinkle each with 1 tbsp cheese.

3. Place on microwave plate and cover with microwave-safe plastic wrap.

4. Microwave on high for 1 minute or until heated through and cheese has melted.

5. If desired, serve with mild salsa for added veggies and taste.

Number of Servings: 4

Teriyaki Chicken Burgers

You can substitute a "lettuce bun" for a bread bun, for those moms going low-carb.

Ingredients

1 lb. lean ground chicken
1 cup corn flakes cereal
1 tsp grated gingerroot
1 tsp soy sauce
½ tsp sesame oil
2 green onions, chopped
1 garlic clove, minced

Directions

1. Heat grill or non-stick pan.

2. In a large bowl, combine all of the ingredients and mix well.

3. Shape mixture into 4-6 patties.

4. Grill or fry 8-10 minutes or until burgers are no longer pink in the middle, turning at least once.

5. Serve on a whole wheat bun, garnish with pineapple slices and/or sliced green onions.

Number of Servings: 4-6

Baked Herb Chicken

My kids love this recipe ~ no leftovers on this one! ~
Contributed by April Gremillion

Ingredients

1 pound uncooked boneless, skinless chicken breasts (about 4 oz each)**
1 tsp olive oil
2 tsp fresh lemon juice, or more to taste***
2 tsp rosemary, fresh, chopped
2 tsp parsley, fresh, chopped
1/4 cups canned chicken broth

Directions

1. Preheat oven to 400 degrees. Coat a small roasting pan with cooking spray.

2. Season both sides of chicken with salt and pepper. Transfer chicken to pan and drizzle with oil, sprinkle with lemon juice, rosemary and parsley. Pour broth around chicken to coat bottom of pan.

3. Bake until chicken is cooked through, about 30 minutes. Garnish with fresh lemons and serve!

Number of Servings: 4

**I used chicken tenderloins because they cook faster and, I think, don't dry out like breasts do. You'll have to adjust cooking time if you choose to use those.

***I simply sliced a lemon in half and squeezed over chicken.

Hot Dog Sandwich

Don't laugh (I know you want to!). I've been eating these since I was a kid. I serve them to Lexi and her friends and they can't get enough! I serve these with the 10-minute baked beans. ~ Honorée

Ingredients

2 slices of home-made honey whole wheat bread
2 turkey or chicken hot dogs, cut in half lengthwise
Ketchup
Mustard
Mayo
Sweet pickle relish

Directions

1. Heat hot dogs and cut them lengthwise.

2. Put on one slice of bread. Add condiments.

3. Watch how fast they're gone!

Number of Servings: 1

Easy Sausage Soup

This soup is a very quick to make -- serve with cornbread and a side salad for complete meal.

Ingredients

16 oz. Kielbasa sausage, reduced-fat
1 can condensed cream of potato soup
1 can condensed split pea and ham soup
1 can diced Italian tomatoes, undrained
1 soup can of water

Directions

1. Cut sausage into cubes and brown in soup pot on medium-high heat.

2. Add remaining ingredients and heat until warm all the way through.

3. Prepare cornbread as package directs.

Number of Servings: 6

White Bean Chicken Chili

This delicious thick chili takes just 20 minutes from start to finish. Top it with some green salsa and crumbled blue tortilla chips. You can certainly add more vegetables to the recipe - I like chopped green bell peppers. ~Honorée

Ingredients

2 15 oz. cans of Great Northern beans, rinsed and drained
2 cups cubed cooked chicken
2 cups low-sodium chicken broth
4 oz. can chopped green chillies, undrained
¼ tsp. each white pepper & salt
½ cup. Low-fat sour cream
2 Tbsp. all-purpose flour

Directions

1. Place one can of drained beans in heavy saucepan and mash slightly. Add remaining ingredients except sour cream and flour. Bring to a boil, then reduce heat, cover, and simmer soup for 15 minutes.

2. In small bowl combine sour cream and flour and mix with wire whisk.

3. Spoon in some of the hot broth from the soup and mix until smooth. Add this mixture to the soup and stir.

4. Cook and stir for a few minutes until thickened, and serve along with more sour cream to top chili.

Number of Servings: 4

Ham & Cheese Calzones

My daughter loves to help make these. They're great for family night. ~Honorée

Ingredients

1 can Pillsbury refrigerated pizza crust, thin crust
24 slices Honey Ham (shaved or sliced very thin)
1 c. shredded 2% cheese, either Cheddar or Colby-jack
1/4 c. fat free ranch dressing
1 tomato, cut into slices

Directions

1. Heat oven to 400°F.

2. Unroll pizza dough on lightly floured surface. Pat dough out to form large rectangle. Cut into 6 equal sections. Top dough with ham.

3. Mix dressing & cheese. Spread on ham. Top with tomatoes. Fold each rectangle in half and seal edges with a fork. Put on baking sheet.

4. Bake 16-18 minutes. Makes 6 calzones.

Number of Servings: 6

Easy Beef Stroganoff

I substitute ground turkey in this recipe and make instant biscuits and a quick salad for a complete meal. ~Honorée

Ingredients

1 lb ground beef cooked and drained
1 cup light sour cream
1 can 98% fat-free cream of mushroom soup
1 can 98% fat-free cream of celery soup
1 medium onion, finely chopped
1 sm. jar or can sliced mushrooms drained (optional)
1 pkg. egg noodles - cooked and drained

Directions

1. In large non-stick skillet, brown beef over medium-high heat. While beef is browning, cook egg noodles in separate pan.

2. Once beef is browned, add onions. When onions are soft, add both cans of soup. Mix well and add mushrooms.

3. Cook for 5 minutes, bringing to boil. Stir in sour cream. Cook for additional 5 minutes.

4. Pour beef mixture over egg noodles and serve.

Number of Servings: 6

Tori's Lavash Pizza

Another great recipe from my sister, and all of the ingredients are from Trader Joe's. ~Contributed by Paige Candee

Ingredients

1 piece of lavash bread
2 tbsp. shredded low-fat mozzarella or Quattro formaggio cheese
1 slice vine-ripened tomato
1 piece prosciutto or diced piece of pesto chicken sausage
1 leaf of arugula
Fresh lemon juice

Directions

1. Heat oven to 350° F.

2. Layer bread with pesto, then light layer of cheese, prosciutto or chicken sausage, and tomatoes.

3. Bake for 10 minutes. Remove from oven, cover with arugula and lemon juice.

Number of Servings: 1

Beef and Spanish Rice

This is a favorite of mine from my younger years. It tastes like you put a ton of effort into it, but it really couldn't be easier. ~Honorée

Ingredients

1 ½ lb. extra-lean ground beef
½ cup onion, chopped
1 10 oz. can diced tomatoes & chilies
1 cup Bush's Black Beans
1 cup water
½ each chili powder, garlic powder, and oregano
1 cup white rice

Directions

1. Brown ground beef and chopped onion in a large non-stick skillet over medium-high heat until meat is browned and onions are soft.

2. Drain in colander, pat dry with a paper towel and clean pan with paper towel.

3. Return meat mixture to pan, stir in remaining ingredients. Bring to a boil; cover, reduce heat and simmer for 20 minutes or until rice is tender, stirring occasionally.

4. Option: serve over Uncle Ben's instant long-grain brown rice.

Number of Servings: 6

Pasta e Fagioli

A yummy Italian favorite.

Ingredients

½ cup onions, diced
2 cloves garlic
1 16 oz. can Italian-style crushed tomatoes
1 14 oz. can northern beans, drained and rinsed
1 cup frozen mixed vegetables
1 cup couscous
4 cups broth (chicken or vegetarian)

Directions

1. In a large non-stick saucepan, over medium-high heat, saute onions and garlic until soft.

2. Add all other ingredients.

3. Bring to a boil, cover, and lower heat. Simmer for 10 minutes.

4. Serve with bread and butter.

Number of Servings: 4

Easy Chicken Cacciatore

A family favorite that doesn't take hours to make. Thank goodness!

Ingredients

6 oz. whole-wheat bow-tie pasta
2 chicken breasts
1 cup Prego spaghetti sauce with basil
2 tbsp olive oil
1 tsp basil, thyme and other "Italian" seasoning to taste
4 oz. dry sherry or brandy

Directions

1. Pre-heat oven to 350°F.

2. Cook pasta according to directions. While pasta water is warming, lightly sautée chicken in olive oil.

3. Add seasoning and sherry to chicken.

4. After chicken is fully cooked, add sauce to pan and heat thoroughly.

5. Keep warm until pasta is ready. Drain pasta and rinse in cool water.

6. Add all ingredients to deep baking dish. Bake for 5-10 minutes.

7. Allow to cool before serving.

Number of Servings: 6

Optional: Add fresh tomatoes, mushrooms, or other veggies to the sautée pan while chicken is cooking or in the baking dish just prior to baking. You can also add cheese prior to baking and remove from oven when cheese begins to bubble.

Shrimp Scampi

This is a low fat, low calorie Shrimp Scampi. Goes great with yellow rice, salad and asparagus.

Ingredients

2 tsp. olive oil
28 large, raw shrimp
3 cloves garlic, diced (or to your taste)
1/3 cup white wine
Salt & pepper to taste
1 tbsp. lemon juice
¼ cup parsley

Directions

1. Heat oil in large non-stick skillet over medium-high heat. Add shrimp, sauté 1 minute. Add garlic; sauté 1 minute.

2. Stir in white wine, salt and pepper; bring mixture to a boil.

3. Reduce heat to medium; cook 30 seconds. Add parsley and juice; toss well to coat. Cook 1 minute or until shrimp is done.

Number of Servings: 4 (Serving size is about 7 shrimp.)

Honey and Soy-Glazed Salmon

This will get your kids eating salmon!

Ingredients

2 4-6 oz. salmon filets
2 tbsp. honey
2 tbsp. low-sodium soy sauce
1 ½ tablespoons lime juice
2 tsp. mustard
1 tbsp. water
2 tsp. vegetable oil

Directions

1. In a small bowl, whisk together honey, soy sauce, lime juice, mustard, and water.

2. In a small non-stick skillet heat oil over moderately high heat until hot but not smoking and cook salmon 2 to 3 minutes on each side, or until golden and cooked through.

3. Transfer salmon to 2 plates. Add honey glaze to skillet and simmer, stirring 1 minute. Pour glaze over salmon. Serve with the starch and veggies of your choice. Enjoy!

Number of Servings: 2

Amazing Chicken Cordon Bleu

This is so amazing, you won't believe it!

Ingredients

2 chicken breasts
½ c. melted butter
1 cup bread crumbs
2 slices ham
2 slices cheese

Directions

1. Pound chicken breast into a "thin" slice. The best way is to cover with thick Saran Wrap and use a mallet, but the back of a large serving spoon does well.

2. Dip each piece of chicken in butter, then into bread crumbs.

3. Place 1 slice ham and cheese on each piece of chicken, roll up and secure with a toothpick.

4. Microwave 4 minutes per breast. Serve with rice, veggies and salad for a quick and delicious wonderful meal.

Number of Servings: 2

Turkey Enchiladas

Healthy and delicious!

Ingredients

2 lb. lean ground turkey
2 10 oz. cans enchilada sauce
1 ½ cups shredded Mexican-style cheese
8 8-inch whole-wheat tortillas

Directions

1. Heat oven to 375°F.

2. Spray a 13x9 glass baking dish with non-stick spray.

3. In 10-inch skillet, brown turkey over medium-high heat, stirring occasionally, until thoroughly cooked; drain. Stir in sauce, reserving about ¼ cup .

4. Place reserved sauce in bottom of pan. Layer tortillas, meat mixture and cheese. Repeat until you've used all of the ingredients and end with cheese.

5. Bake 15 minutes or until hot.

Number of Servings: 6-8

Best Chicken Salad Ever!

Both my kids and I love this easy to make chicken salad with fruits that are available year-round. This recipe can be easily cut in half, so you can use the rotisserie chicken for dinner and use the leftovers for this salad (great for lunch the next day!). My son is not a big fan of meat/chicken, but he can't get enough of this! ~ Contributed by Kelly Russell

Ingredients

4 cups rotisserie chicken, cut into bite-size pieces (my favorite is the lemon garlic chicken)
2 cups sliced celery
2 cups whole seedless grapes, sliced in half
2 cups diced apples
2 cups pineapple tidbits
1 cup sliced almonds (I use Sunkist honey roasted almonds)
1 cup mayo

Directions

1. Mix all ingredients in large bowl.

2. Chill 1-3 hours.

3. Eat and enjoy!

Number of Servings: 4

Vegetarian Recipes

Saffron Rice, Beans and Peas

Quick, easy, delicious.

Ingredients

1 5 oz. Package Saffron Yellow Rice
1 can black or red beans
1 cup frozen peas

Directions

1. Cook rice according to stove-top or microwave directions, about 20 minutes.

2. Heat beans in microwave for 3-5 minutes while rice is cooking.

3. Mix rice and beans. Add frozen peas and stir. Let sit about 3 minutes before serving.

4. Number of Servings: 2-4

Note: This recipe can also be made with chicken or shrimp.

Black Bean Cakes

This recipe is one I used to expand Lexi's palette. She enjoys making these "pancakes". ~Honorée

Ingredients

1 15-oz. can black beans, undrained
1 cup salsa
2 tbsp. lime juice
1 8½ oz. package corn bread mix
½ cup dairy sour cream Mexican-style dip

Directions

1. In a medium bowl, slightly mash undrained beans. Stir in ½ cup of salsa and lime juice. Stir in corn bread mix just until moistened.

2. Coat a large non-stick skillet with non-stick cooking spray and heat over medium heat.

3. Spoon ¼ cup of batter into hot skillet. Use the back of a spoon to spread batter into a 4-inch circle. Cook for 1-2 minutes on each side or until browned.

4. Serve each cake with equal parts of remaining salsa and sour cream dip.

Number of Servings: 4

Orange Dream Fruit Salad

Make this the first beautiful day of spring, and you'll make it many times throughout the spring and summer.

Ingredients

1 cup chopped, peeled, seeded mango or papaya.
1 11-oz. can mandarin orange sections, drained
1 cup seedless red and/or green grapes, halved
½ cup orange-flavored yogurt
¼ tsp. poppy seeds

Directions

1. In a medium-sized bowl, combine mango, orange sections, and grapes.

2. In a small bowl, stir together yogurt and poppy seeds.

3. Combine mixtures and serve!

Number of Servings: 4

Note: This recipe can also be made with chicken or shrimp.

Vegetable-Cheese Chowder

Perfect for a cold fall or winter evening.

Ingredients

1 16-oz. package frozen broccoli, cauliflower, and carrots
½ cup water
2 cups 1%-2% milk
1/3 cup all-purpose flour
1 14-oz. can low-sodium chicken broth
4 oz. 2% shredded smoked or regular Gouda cheese

Directions

1. In a large saucepan, combine vegetables and water. Bring to boil and reduce heat. Simmer, covered, for aobut 4 minutes or until veggies are just tender. Do not drain.

2. While veggies are simmering, combine 2/3 cup of milk and the flour and mix well.

3. Add to saucepan, then add remaining milk and chicken broth. Cook and stir until thickened and bubbly. Cook for 1 more minute.

4. Add cheese and cook and stir over low heat until cheese is melted.

Number of Servings: 4

Bean, Corn & Avocado Salad

Light and tasty!

Ingredients

1 can black beans, drained
1 can yellow sweet corn, drained
1 medium red-ripe tomato
½ cup chopped raw onions
1 avocado, cubed
2 oz. lime juice
1 tsp. olive oil

Directions

1. In a large bowl, mix beans and corn. Add onion, tomato and avocado.

2. Season with lime juice and olive oil.

3. Add salt & pepper to taste and serve.

Number of Servings: 4-6

Pesto and Cheese Tomato Melt

Ready in 12 minutes, and so flavorful!

Ingredients

¼ cup purchase basil pesto
2 tbsp. chopped walnuts
4 1-inch slices sourdough French bread, toasted
¼ cup oil-packed diced tomatoes, drained and chopped
4 oz. 2% shredded mozzarella cheese

Directions

1. Pre-heat oven on broil.

2. In a small bow, stir together pesto and nuts. Spread mixture over bread slices.

3. Top with tomatoes and cheese.

4. Broil 4 inches from the heat for 2-3 minutes or until cheese melts.

Number of Servings: 2

Ravioli with Veggies

Kids love ravioli. Moms love it when their kids eat veggies. Here's a solution!

Ingredients

1 9 oz. package refrigerated cheese-filled ravioli
4 cups julienned, diced and cut veggies: use red bell peppers, zucchini, peas, lima beans and corn*
½ tsp garlic powder
¼ cup water
½ teaspoon chicken-flavored instant bouillon
Salt & pepper to taste
1 oz. (¼ cup) shredded reduced-fat mozzarella

Directions

1. Cook ravioli according to package directions.

2. While ravioli is cooking, heat large non-stick skillet with non-stick cooking spray over medium-high heat until hot.

3. Add veggies, garlic and salt and pepper. Cook 3-5 minutes or until vegetables are crisp-tender.

4. Drain ravioli and rinse with hot water. Add ravioli, water and bouillon to veggies. Cook over medium head an additional 3-5 minutes or until thoroughly heated. Add cheese, toss and serve.

Number of Servings: 4

Tostadas

I've been making and eating these since I was a kid. They are quick and delicious. ~ Honorée

Ingredients

4 corn tostadas
1 can vegetarian refried beans
1 medium tomato, diced
1 large avocado, "smooshed"
1 tbsp mayonnaise or Nayonaise (soy mayo)
Taco sauce
1 oz. (¼ cup) shredded reduced-fat mozzarella

Directions

1. Heat tostada shell in oven. This makes them extra crispy.

2. Heat refried beans in a medium sauce pan until easy to stir.

3. Mix avocado and mayo for a creamy "mock guac".

4. Spread beans onto tostada, top with tomato, mock guac, taco sauce and cheese. Eat. Repeat.

Number of Servings: 4

Slow Cooker Recipes

Mexican Slow Cooker Chicken

Yummy and easy, two of my favorite things. ~ Honorée

Ingredients

3 chicken breasts (about 1 ¼ to 1 ½ lbs.)
1 can diced tomatoes (do not drain)
1 can black beans (do not drain)
1 can Mexican chili beans (do not drain)
1 pkg taco seasoning
1 can black olives
1 can chopped green chilies

Directions

1. Layer chicken in bottom of Slow Cooker. Add the rest of the ingredients in the order written.

2. Do not stir. Cook on low 7-8 hours.

3. Take out chicken and shred. Return chicken to Slow Cooker and stir well.

4. Serve with tortilla chips or on a flour tortilla.

5. Serve with chopped lettuce, tomatoes, and shredded cheese if desired.

Number of Servings: 6

Mushroom Beef Slow Cooker

Yummy and easy, two of my favorite things. ~ Honorée

Ingredients

1 lb. organic lean beef stew meat
1 can 98% fat-free cream of mushroom soup
½ cup water
1 pkt. Dry onion soup mix
8 oz. fresh mushrooms, sliced

Directions

1. Brown meat in skillet over med-high heat. You can skip this step to save time and the recipe will still be great. I just think it gives the meat more flavor and helps it hold together better.

2. Place meat in 4 quart Slow Cooker. Place mushrooms on top of beef.

3. Combine soup, water and soup mix and pour over mushrooms and beef.

4. Cook on low for 6-8 hours or high for 3-4 hours.

5. Tastes great over brown rice or hot cooked noodles.

Number of Servings: 6

Slow Cooker Chicken & Stuffing

You can also make this with turkey, the Cauliflower Mock Mashed Potatoes and a can of cranberries for a non-Thanksgiving Thanksgiving meal!

Ingredients

6 whole boneless, skinless chicken breasts (about 3 lbs.)
1 can 98% fat-free cream of mushroom soup
1 box Stove-Top stuffing mix or bag or pre-seasoned stuffing mix
½ cup chicken broth (or water)

Directions

1. Spray your Slow Cooker with cooking spray. Add chicken breasts.

2. Combine stuffing, soup and liquid. Spread over chicken.

3. Cook on low 6-8 hours.

Number of Servings: 6

Slow Cooker Chili

This can also be made on the stove. Just make sure you're around to stir it occasionally …

P.S. I know this has more than 7 ingredients, but I made the exception because its just lots of cans to open and pour … and enjoy!

Ingredients

1 lb. ground turkey, chicken or beef
1 cup chopped onions
1 can each: kidney beans, northern beans, petite diced tomatoes, tomato sauce (dump in with all of the juices)
1 tsp garlic powder
1 bell pepper, chopped
1 cup chopped celery
1 pkg. chili seasonings
Salt & pepper to taste

Directions

1. Brown meat in a large skillet. Add celery, onion and bell pepper, cook until almost done. Drain and place in Slow Cooker.

2. Add remaining ingredients to Slow Cooker and stir to mix.

3. Cook on low 6-8 hours.

Number of Servings: 6

Slow Cooker Barbecue Chicken

In a word, yum!

Ingredients

6 pieces of chicken thighs
1 bottle BBQ sauce
1 tsp salt
2 tsp cayenne pepper

Directions

1. Put all of the ingredients in the Slow Cooker and mix well.

2. Cook on low 6-8 hours.

Great with a green salad.

Number of Servings: 6

Pot Roast a la Slow Cooker

This is a great recipe to eat and then freeze in appropriate portions for a quick heat-and-eat later.

Ingredients

2 ½ lb. chuck roast
2 large potatoes, chopped
4 ½ cups of carrots, sliced
3 cups chicken or beef broth
½ large onion, diced
Season to taste

Directions

1. Brown beef.

2. Cut veggies and add to Slow Cooker.

3. Add beef, broth and seasonings.

4. Cook on low 8-10 hours.

Number of Servings: 10 (great for left-overs!)

Crockery Pot Potato Soup

From our friends to the north, Candice Brown of Brandon, Manitoba, Canada.

Ingredients

6-8 potatoes, cut into chunks
2 medium carrots, cubed
2 ribs of celery, cubed
1 medium onion, chopped
1 tbsp. parsley flakes
5 cups of water
1 can of evaporated milk

Directions

1. Put all ingredients into the crockery pot, mix well.

2. Cook in crockery pot on low for 8 hours or until everything is cooked through.

3. One hour before serving, add evaporated milk.

Number of Servings: 4

No Peek Beef Casserole

One more from our friends to the north, Candice Brown of Brandon, Manitoba, Canada.

Ingredients

2 lbs. stew meat
1 envelope of onion soup
1 10 oz. can cream of mushroom soup
1 4 oz. can of mushrooms

Directions

1. Combine all ingredients in Slow Cooker and stir together well.

2. Cover and cook on low 8-12 hours on high 4-5 hours.

3. Serve over noodles or rice.

Number of Servings: 4-6

Slow Cooker Chicken Taco

It's so simple and perfect for working single moms! Tasty, healthy and low in fat and calories. ~Contributed by Paige Candee

Ingredients

3 chicken breasts
1 jar of your favorite salsa
6-8 whole wheat tortillas
Taco toppings as desired: cheese, lettuce, tomato, sour cream, green chilis, etc.

Directions

1. Put chicken breasts in Slow Cooker with salsa.

2. Cover and put on low heat for 6-8 hours or high heat for 3-4 hours. The chicken will shred when stirred.

3. Serve on tortillas with toppings.

Number of Servings: 6-8

Slow Cooker Oatmeal

You'll love waking up to the smell of this! This recipe is very satisfying, the cooking method makes it very creamy (no need for milk) and the fruit makes it sweet (no need for added sugar or sweetener!) Your kids will love this, and you'll love that they have something in their tummies as they start the day.

Ingredients

1 cup steel cut oats (not rolled oats)
4 cups water
1 large or 2 small apples, peeled, cored and chopped
½ cup raisins
1 tbsp. cinnamon
1 tsp. vanilla extract

Directions

1. Place all ingredients in slow-cooker and stir to mix. Turn on low and leave overnight. I use a small 2 quart crockpot, but I have also made it in a large one.

2. Wake up and eat!

Number of Servings: 6

Lunches from Home

Tuna Sandwiches

You can serve this in a pita, a spoonful on crackers, or even on a rice cake. Yummy!

Ingredients

1 can tuna packed in water
1 tbsp each sweet pickle relish and mayo
1 tsp minced fresh onion
½ stalk of celery, diced
2 slices whole wheat bread

Directions

1. Drain can of tuna. In medium bowl, mix tuna, relish, mayo, onion and celery.

2. Spread onto bread and make into a sandwich.

3. You can make a tuna melt by using 1 slice of bread, topped with tuna and a slice of cheese, broiled in oven at 450°F for about 7-10 minutes.

4. You can also mix in any or all of the following for variations on this favorite: cucumbers, carrots, water chestnuts, green, yellow or red peppers, lettuce and tomato.

Number of Servings: 1

*You can substitute any meat and cheese slices

Munchables

A yummy alternative to pre-packaged lunchables. ~Kyle Benjamin Johnson, age 7

Ingredients

1 thick slice of ham or turkey
1 thick slice Monterey jack cheese
5 crackers
1 healthy fruit wrap
3 paper cupcake containers
1 French fry tray
1 sticker

Directions

1. Cut the meat and cheese with your child's favorite cookie cutter, such as a flower, star, or circle. Put in two of the cupcake holders.

2. Add sticker to the fruit roll-up, then add to the last cupcake holder.

3. Be sure to stick an "I love you" note in there somewhere.

Number of Servings: 1

*You can substitute any meat and cheese slices

Turkey & Cheese Wrap

Stays "just made" in your child's lunchbox.

Ingredients

1 6-8 oz. wheat wheat tortilla
3 slices turkey*
1 tbsp each mustard and mayo
2 slices 2% cheddar cheese*

Honorée's daughter Lexi loves tomatoes, which tend to make the whole thing mushy by lunchtime. Slice the tomatoes and put in separate baggie or aluminum foil.

Directions

1. Spread mustard and mayo onto tortilla.

2. Add meat and cheese.

3. Roll it up, put it in a plastic bag, and it will be ready to eat come lunchtime!

Number of Servings: 1

*You can substitute any meat and cheese slices

Quick Egg Salad

You'll want to boil the eggs and let them cool completely, then proceed with the recipe.

Ingredients

6 hard boiled eggs
4 tbsp fat-free mayo
3 tbsp yellow mustard
2 tsp sweet pickle relish
1 tsp minced fresh onions
Sprinkle of paprika, just to make it pretty
Fresh tomato, sliced

Directions

1. Chop up eggs.

2. In a medium bowl, add eggs, mayo, mustard, relish and onions. Mix well.

3. To make an open-faced sandwich, spread mixture onto bread and add tomato. Salt & pepper to taste. For a full sandwich, just add another piece of bread on top of the whole thing. Enjoy!

Number of Servings: 4

Not-so-Sloppy Sloppy Joes

You can serve these warm at home, then let them cool and send them to school!

Ingredients

1 lb. lean ground turkey
1 pkg. McCormick Sloppy Joe Mix
1 6 oz. can tomato paste
1 ¼ cups water

Directions

1. Brown ground turkey in large skillet on medium heat. Drain fat.

2. Stir in seasoning mix, tomato paste and water.

3. Bring contents to a boil, reduce heat and simmer 10 minutes. Stir occasionally.

Number of Servings: 8

Bagel Sandwich

A great sandwich alternative.

Ingredients

1 tbsp light cream cheese
1 whole wheat bagel, split and toasted
1 slice cheese
2 slices dill pickle
¼ cup shredded carrots
1 leaf lettuce

Directions

1. Spread cream cheese onto bagel.

2. Put all of the other ingredients on the bagel.

3. It's a big mouthful, so cut into 4 pieces and enjoy!

Number of Servings: 1

Turkey and Cheese Rolls

A great quick lunch for the kids, a low-carb snack for mom. Take them to go in a small plastic container.

Ingredients

4 slices of your favorite organic lunch meat
1 slice deli-style cheese
1 oz. cream cheese
2 lettuce leaves
1 dill pickle spear
Yellow or brown mustard (optional)

Directions

1. Fold cheese slice into quarters.

2. Cut pickle into quarters

3. Halve each of your lettuce leaves

4. Lay out the lettuce, add mustard at one end of the lettuce leaf, top with 1 piece of meat each, then piece of cheese, spread on cream cheese, top with pickle and roll it up.

Number of Servings: 1

Snack & Side Ideas

I would always run out of ideas for "what else do I put in the box," which meant Lexi would get the same thing day in and day out. I knew I wouldn't like that myself, so I created this list of snacks. I let her choose from the list what she thinks she would like in the coming week and that way it's always a little different.

Fruit: Grapes
Bananas,
Oranges
Strawberries
Cut apples

Veggies: Carrots or broccoli with ranch dressing
Cucumbers
Celery with peanut butter and raisins

Other stuff:String cheese and crackers
Peanuts and raisins
Pretzels
Cheezits
Squeezable yogurts
Cottage cheese and fruit, such as pineapple or peaches

Veggies & Side Dishes They Will Eat!
Rice & Peas

A simple to make side that replaces a veggie and a starch. Since rice and peas combine to make a complete protein, this is also a tasty vegetarian main dish.

Ingredients

1 cup cooked rice ~ to stay under 20 minutes, use instant brown rice
1 cup frozen peas
1 small can mushrooms, including liquid
3 tbs. butter
½ tsp. garlic salt
½ tsp. black pepper

Directions

1. Combine all ingredients in a saucepan to heat on stovetop at medium setting. Stir gently until well-blended and creamy, to avoid crushing the peas.

2. Alternate method: Combine all ingredients into a covered glass casserole. Heat in microwave for up to 10 minutes (depending on strength of oven), stirring 3 times while cooking.

Number of Servings: 4

Brussels Sprouts

Be sure to cook the exact amount of time recommended, otherwise they release sulfur and smell like something your kids won't want to eat ...

Ingredients

18 - Brussel Sprouts, fresh
1 - Lemon, halved
1 - Tbsp Olive Oil
1 - Tbsp Butter
Salt & pepper to taste

Directions

1. In a very high heat frying pan, add olive oil.

2. Cut the sprouts in half, notch out the core and slice them very thin, like cabbage. Throw in the Brussels Sprouts, squeeze in 1/2 the lemon (through a strainer to catch pits), add salt and pepper to taste and cook exactly 60 seconds.

3. Remove from heat, add the other 1/2 lemon, stir in butter and serve.

Number of Servings: 4

Sweet Orange Asparagus

Just sweet enough they'll eat it and love it!

Ingredients

1 lb. fresh asparagus spears, trimmed
¼ cup orange juice
1 tsp grated orange peel
½ tsp cornstarch
Dash pepper

Directions

1. In a large skillet, bring ½ inch water to a boil. Add asparagus; return to boil. Cover and cook 3-5 minutes until asparagus is tender.*

2. In a small non-stick saucepan, combine orange juice, peel, cornstarch and pepper; mix well. Cook over medium heat until mixture boils and begins to thicken. Remove from heat.

3. Drain asparagus; place on serving platter.

Number of Servings: 4

*You could also steam the veggies in a steamer. This also takes just 3-5 minutes.

Glazed Carrots

My daughter (who "hates" carrots) eats these until they are gone!
~Honorée

Ingredients

3 medium carrots, sliced
1 tbsp butter or ghee (purified butter)
1.5 tbsp brown sugar

Directions

1. Cook carrots covered in small amounts of boiling water about 6-10 minutes or until tender. Drain.

2. In a skillet melt butter over low heat, then add brown sugar. Stir until melted.

3. Add carrots, stir until glazed.

4. Season if desired, and serve.

Number of Servings: 3-4

Cauliflower "Mashed Potatoes"

Shhh! The kids won't know they aren't indulging on mashed potatoes.

Ingredients

3 ½ cups of raw cauliflower, steamed to soft
¼ cup skim milk
2 tsp fat-free sour cream
1 tsp Neufchatel (low-fat) cream cheese
2 tsp butter, separated

Directions

1. While cauliflower is steaming, mix milk, sour cream, cream cheese and 1 tsp butter.

2. Use hand-mixer or blender on cauliflower to create desired consistency.

3. Add milk mixture and stir until completely mixed.

4. Add 1 tsp butter, salt and pepper to taste and serve.

Number of Servings: 4

10-Minute Baked Beans

So quick and yet so delicious!

Ingredients

1 15 oz. can no-salt-added kidney or pinto beans, drained
3 tbsp brown sugar
2 tbsp onion flakes
¼ cup BBQ sauce

Directions

1. In a medium saucepan, combine all ingredients.

2. Bring to boil, cover, reduce heat and cook 5 minutes.

3. Uncover and cook additional 5 minutes.

4. Eat!

Number of Servings: 4

Two-Apple Coleslaw

Get fruits and veggies into your kids in an easy way.

Ingredients

¾ cup Light Miracle Whip Dressing
1 tbsp honey
16 oz. package pre-cut and diced coleslaw blend
1 medium red apple, chopped
1 medium green apple, chopped

Directions

1. Mix dressing and honey in a bowl.

2. Add rest of the ingredients and stir.

3. For best results, refrigerate at least 20-30 minutes before serving.

Number of Servings: 4

Sweet Potato Fries

These can accompany any number of burgers, sandwiches or dishes.

Ingredients

4 sweet potatoes, peeled and cut lengthwise like steak fries (about 10 per potato)
3 tbsp olive oil
3 tsp taco seasoning, low-sodium option

Directions

1. Preheat oven to 425°F.

2. In a large mixing bowl, drizzle oil over the potatoes. Add taco seasoning mix and toss to coat.

3. Place fries in one even layer on cookie sheet sprayed with non-stick spray.

4. Bake 10 minutes, turn and bake 10 more minutes. Fries should be soft on the inside and crispy on the outside.

Number of Servings: 6

Sautéed Broccoli with Garlic and Almonds

My son loves broccoli, and this is one of the ways I make it for him. ~Contributed by Lori Johnson

Ingredients

1 head broccoli, chopped
1 clove garlic
2 tbsp. olive oil
Parmesan Cheese, to taste

Directions

1. Put broccoli in microwave-safe dish, cover with ¼ inch of water and plastic wrap. Place in microwave on HIGH for 2 minutes.

2. While broccoli is cooking, sautée garlic in olive oil in a large non-stick skillet on medium-high high.

3. Add broccoli and sautée until tender.

4. Sprinkle with parmesan cheese. Add salt and pepper to taste.

Number of Servings: 2-4

Cheesy Zucchini Sticks

Breads crumbs and parmesan cheese make the zucchini go down!

Ingredients

1 large zucchini
2 tbsp Progresso Italian Bread Crumbs
2 tbsp Shredded Parmesan Cheese
1 tsp salt
1 tsp pepper
1 tbsp garlic powder
Cooking spray

Directions

1. Cut zucchini into thirds then each third into 8 wedges.

2. Arrange in baking dish (9x12x2). Spray with cooking spray.

3. Season with seasonings. Top with bread crumbs and parmesan cheese.

4. Bake at 350°F for 15 minutes or until zucchini is tender.

Number of Servings: 4 servings of 6 sticks

Snacks, Sweet Treats & Desserts

Peanut-Butter Balls

These peanut butter balls are simply delicious ~ full of protein, can be added to lunch or used as a quick after-school snack.

Ingredients

1 cup freshly-ground peanut butter*
1 cup vanilla protein powder**
½ cup honey
Optional: finely-chopped almonds or walnuts

Directions

1. Mix peanut butter, protein powder and honey.

2. Use 1 tbsp mixture to roll into balls.

3. Refrigerate about 30 minutes.

4. Optional: roll in nuts to add crunch and some additional protein.

Number of Servings: 2-4

*Honorée gets hers from Whole Foods and grinds it herself.
**Honorée uses Shaklee's Instant Protein Soy Mix, Natural Flavor. www.shaklee.com

Juice Popsicles

You can buy the molds from Tupperware or Target. You can also use plastic or paper cups ~ just wait until the juice hardens a little bit before you put the popsicle sticks in.

Ingredients

24 oz. juice of your choice
6 popsicle molds and sticks

Directions

1. Pour juice into molds.

2. Freeze for 4 hours or overnight.

Number of Servings: 6

17-Minute Peanut Butter Cookies

For the moms ~ this will satisfy your sweet tooth (and curb any cravings). For the kids ~ they will love how quick and easy they are, as well as yummy!

Ingredients

1 cup peanut butter (use fresh ground peanuts from Whole Foods or the commercial peanut butter of your choice)
1 cup organic granulated sugar
1 egg

Directions

1. Pre-heat oven to 325°F.

2. Mix all ingredients together in a medium-sized bowl.

3. Drop teaspoon-sized dollop onto cooking stone or greased cookie sheet.

4. Bake for 8-12 minutes and try to let them cool before eating.

Number of Servings: 14

Blueberries and Cream

I thought, "No way is this going to be good with sour cream!" and I was wrong! It is incredibly delicious. My daughter asks for it all the time. ~Honorée

Ingredients

1 pint fresh blueberries (about 1 cup)
1/3 cup low-fat sour cream
3 tbsp brown sugar
1/3 tsp pure vanilla extract
Pinch salt

Directions

1. Mix all of the ingredients together.

2. Refrigerate in 2 separate bowls or teacups for about 20-30 minutes.

3. Enjoy!

4. Warning: This is so delicious, you'll probably want to make it again tomorrow. (Don't say I didn't warn you!)

Number of Servings: 2

Brownies

These are made in the microwave, so they are quick and easy.

Ingredients

2 large eggs
1 cup organic granulated white sugar
3 tsp vanilla
½ tsp salt
¾ cup organic bread flour (I use King Arthur)
½ cup butter, melted
½ cup cocoa, unsweetened
1 cup walnuts (optional)

Directions

1. Beat eggs with sugar, salt & vanilla for 1 minute. Pour in melted butter.

2. Add flour, cocoa and nuts. Mix all together, then pour into an 8X8 microwavable pan and microwave on high for 6 minutes. Turn pan every 3 minutes for even cooking.

3. Serve after cooled. It is pretty good with a little ice-cream on the side, too.

Number of Servings: 16

Cake for One

From start to first bite is three minutes. It's a snack, it's a dessert, whatever it is, its delicious!

Ingredients

1 tbsp each: whole wheat pastry flour, sugar and oats
Pinch of baking soda
1 tsp cinnamon
2 tbsp plain yogurt
2 tbsp cranberries

Directions

1. Spray a small bowl with cooking spray and add the yogurt to bowl and on top it place your dry ingredients (but not cranberries).

2. Mix well and then mix in cranberries.

3. Place uncovered in microwave and cook on HIGH for one minute*, then enjoy while warm.

Number of Servings: 1

*If its not quite done at a minute, cook it in 10-second increments until done.

(Almost) Cheesecake

This is a fun "slumber party" treat the kids can make themselves.

Ingredients

1 Graham Cracker Square
2 tbsp strawberry or mixed berry preserves
2 tbsp cream cheese
4 slices honey whole wheat bread

Directions

1. On the Graham Cracker square thinly spread the Cream Cheese. Top with strawberry preserve and enjoy your "cheesecake."

Number of Servings: 1

Waffle Shortcake

A personal shortcake your kids can make for themselves (and you).

Ingredients

1 frozen waffle
1/2 cup frozen blueberries or berry of your choice
3 tbsp pressurized whipped cream

Directions

1. Heat waffle in microwave until just thawed, about 30-45 seconds

2. Top with berries and cream.

3. Enjoy!

Number of Servings: 1

Raspberry Cheesecake Sandwich

So fun, quick and delightful! A quick take on a classic favorite.

Ingredients

1 graham cracker, split into two squares
1 oz. fat-free or low-fat cream cheese (I use Neufchatel cheese)
1 TBS Raspberry Jam

Directions

1. Spread the cream cheese on both crackers.

2. Place jam on top of the cream cheese on one cracker, and place the other cracker (cream cheese side down) on top and press gently to make a delicious cheesecake sandwich.

Number of Servings: 2

11-Minute Peanut Butter Fudge

Goodness! How can something so simple be so good?

Ingredients

1 cup Butter, room temperature
1 cup Peanut Butter, smooth or chunky
1 tsp Vanilla Extract
2.75 cups Powdered Sugar, sifted

Directions

1. Mush together the room temperature butter and peanut butter in a larger microwaveable bowl. Microwave uncovered on high for 2 minutes.

2. Carefully remove and stir. Microwave for an additional 2 minutes.

3. Carefully remove and stir in the vanilla. Mix in the sifted powdered sugar.

4. Press into a buttered or sprayed 8x8 glass dish, cover and refrigerate until set.

5. Add chopped nuts if you'd like!

Number of Servings: 64

Breakfast ~ One of the Three Most Important Meals of the Day

Cheesy Eggs with Spinach

Cover up spinach with enough other goodness (cheese) and your kids will eat it. Promise.

Ingredients

3 large eggs
1 cup fresh spinach
¼ cup shredded low-fat cheddar or mozzarella cheese
½ tsp. butter
2 tbsp fat-free Half-and-Half

Directions

1. Whisk eggs and add Half-and-Half

2. Melt butter in large non-stick skillet over medium heath

3. When eggs are almost done, add spinach. Scramble well.

4. Serve with salsa for added flavor.

Number of Servings: 2

Egg in a Hole

Kids love it. Adults love it. It's quick, easy, nutritious and delicious. Especially easy in the morning, also can be a quick, light dinner, too.

Ingredients

1 slice whole grain bread
1 large egg
1 pat of butter

Directions

1. Melt butter in a small nonstick frying pan on medium heat.

2. Cut a 2" hole in the bread and add it (and the "hole") to the pan.

3. Crack an egg into the hole in the bread and fry on medium heat for about 1-1/2 minutes, turn over and fry the other side for another 1-1/2 minutes or to the desired doneness.

Number of Servings: 1

Quick French Toast

There's no sugar added to this recipe to keep it simple and quick and healthy.

Ingredients

2 eggs, beaten
2 tbsp. soy or regular milk
Dash of cinnamon
4 slices honey whole wheat bread

Directions

1. Mix eggs, milk and cinnamon.

2. Dip bread slices individually into mix until lightly coated.

3. Cook in non-stick pan until golden brown.

4. Add powdered sugar or honey to taste.

Number of Servings: 4

Author's Note: You can scramble left-over eggs, the cinnamon and milk makes them taste yummy!

Silver Dollar Pancakes

You loved them as a kid -- and now you can make breakfast fun again with these bite-size pancakes. I make double batches and freeze the pancakes for a quick breakfast.

Note: You can also make these as regular-sized pancakes, adding in additional ingredients like chocolate chips or blueberries.

Ingredients

½ cup all-purpose or bread flour
½ tbsp. sugar
¼ tsp. baking soda
¾ cup buttermilk
1 tablespoon vegetable oil
1 large egg
½ teaspoon vanilla extract

Directions

1. Whisk flour, sugar, and baking soda together in a medium bowl. Make a well in center. Whisk buttermilk, oil, egg, and vanilla together in another bowl until blended. Pour into well and whisk just until moistened. Let stand 5 minutes.

2. Meanwhile, coat a large nonstick skillet with vegetable cooking spray and place over medium heat until hot, but not smoking.

3. For each pancake, pour 1 tablespoon batter into skillet. Cook until bubbles appear all over cakes and begin to burst, about 3 minutes. Turn and cook until undersides are golden, about 1 to 2 minutes more.

Number of Servings: 4

Potato Pancakes

You can grate the potatoes or buy pre-grated ones in the freezer section.

Ingredients

1 cup grated potatoes
1/3 cup milk
1 large egg
1/3 cup flour

Directions

1. Mix all ingredients together in a large bowl.

2. Cook like a pancake, using ½ cup of the mixture at a time.

Number of Servings: 3

Breakfast Burritos

You can wrap these in some tin foil and send them with your kids as they run to the bus!

Ingredients

1 8-inch whole wheat flour tortilla
1 large egg
1 tbsp. salsa
1 slice or 1 tbsp. American cheese
1 tbsp. bacon bits or a link of sausage chopped into pieces

Directions

1. Scramble egg with bacon bits.

2. Wrap in burrito with cheese and salsa.

3. Variations: Use veggies, different kind of cheese, sour cream or sausage.

Number of Servings: 1

Comfort Foods

{Because we all need a little comforting now and then.}

Mac 'n Cheese

This is the healthiest I could get this ~ there's high fiber content from the whole wheat elbows and the kids still love it.

Ingredients

4 oz uncooked whole wheat elbow macaroni
4 wedges Laughing Cow light cheese
Salt and pepper to taste
1-2 TBLSP milk

Directions

1. Cook the elbows according to package directions.

2. Drain almost, but not until totally dry and add the unwrapped Laughing Cow Light wedges, the milk, salt, pepper and stir.

Number of Servings: 2

Grilled Cheese (about) 100 Ways

Grace said, "Honorée, everybody knows how to make grilled cheese." Honorée said, "Grace, kids can eat the same thing every day, especially if they think it's a little bit different (and even if they don't)." Take it away, Gracie!

Grilled cheese is always one of those staples. You've got bread, you've got cheese, you've got butter and a pan, and voila! But grilled cheese doesn't have to just consist of bread and cheese. As a cook in college, Grace first learned to feed her hungry roommates after class with as little as possible, and would custom make grilled cheese sandwiches to order with any vegetables/meats she had on hand to add nutritional value and extra flavor. And of course, a nice hot bowl of tomato soup always makes a grilled cheese sandwich into a warm and comforting meal.

Ingredients

2 slices wheat, white or whatever bread you like
1 tbsp butter
2 slices or 1/3 cup shredded cheese ~ I use 2% cheddar or Veggie Slices Cheddar (American always melts well, but a mix of cheddar and jack are always a nice change)
Option: Use non-stick spray, such as "I Can't Believe Its Not Butter" in the flavor of your choice, in place of butter.

Directions

1. Pre-heat non-stick skillet.
2. Spread softened butter on each bread slice or heat butter in pan over medium-high heat until it melts.
3. Put cheese slices between bread.
4. Cooked until golden brown on each side and cheese is melted.

Number of Servings: 1

This is where the fun comes in: Add these or your other favorite extra ingredients after the cheese has started to melt so it all warms to the same temperature. Make sure these extras are all chopped to bite sized pieces and evenly spaced so no one gets a single bite of just one ingredient.

Vegetables/fruit:
pickled jalapenos
mild green chilies
tomatoes
sliced mushrooms
grilled onions
sun-dried tomatoes
chopped artichoke hearts
avocado
sprouts
green apple slices

Meats:
chopped or whole already cooked leftover bacon
ham
turkey
prosciutto
pancetta
salami
roast beef
Switch up cheeses (stick with soft or semi-soft cheese, hard cheese will not melt well):
provolone
mozzarella
munster
colby
cheddar

monterey Jack
swiss
fontina
gruyere

Get fancy:
spread jarred pesto on the cheese side of the bread
marinated roasted red peppers
grilled caprese: fresh mozzarella, tomato and basil leaves
caramelized onion, brie and slices of apples and/or bacon
croque Monsiuer: ham and Gruyere cheese (or any good melting
cheese, like Fontina), topped with a fried egg
roast beef and cheddar with mild horseradish sauce
brie and green apples

If You Have a Little More Time

Recipes that take a short time to prepare,
and cook a little longer.

Meat Loaf

Prep time: 10 minutes, Ready in 40 minutes

This is a dish that will leave your home smelling delicious and make your kid's taste buds happy!

Ingredients

3/4 lb. extra-lean ground beef or turkey
½ cup Italian-style bread crumbs
1/3 cup chopped green bell pepper
¼ cup ketchup
2 teaspoons onion powder
1 egg or egg white
2 tbsp ketchup

Directions

1. Heat oven to 475°F. Line bread pan with foil or use non-stick cooking spray.

2. In medium bowl, combine all ingredients except 2 tbsp ketchup.

3. Put mixture into pan and spread 2 tbsp ketchup on top.

4. Bake for 20 minutes or until center is no longer pink. Let stand 5 minutes before serving.

Number of Servings: 4

Lasagna

Prep time: 15 minutes, Ready in 50 minutes

Make this dish over the weekend and use it for left-overs during the week.

Ingredients

No-cook lasagna noodles
1 cup low-fat cottage cheese (or substitute ricotta)
1 egg white
2 oz. (½ cup) shredded mozzarella cheese
¼ lb. extra-lean ground beef, ground turkey or Morningstar
Farms Griller Recipe Starters "Ground Beef"
1 (25.5 oz.) jar chunky vegetable spaghetti sauce
¼ cup grated Parmesan cheese

Directions

1. Heat oven to 400°F. Spray 9-inch square pan with non-stick cooking spray.

2. In medium bowl, combine cottage cheese, egg white and ¼ cup of cheese and mix well. Set aside.

3. In large non-stick skillet, brown ground beef over medium-to-high heat; drain. Stir in spaghetti sauce and simmer for 5 minutes.

4. Spread small amount of sauce on bottom of sprayed pan. Layer half each of noodles, cottage cheese mixture and sauce; repeat layers. Top with remaining ¼ cup mozzarella cheese and Parmesan cheese.

5. Bake at 400°F. for 25 to 35 minutes or until lasagna is bubbling and cheese is melted.

Number of Servings: 6

Giant Cheesy Potato Fries

Prep time: 15 minutes, Ready in 1 hour

You can't eat just one!

Ingredients

3 medium russet potatoes, unpeeled, cut lengthwise into 8
wedges
2 tsp olive oil
¼ tsp dried Italian seasoning
1/8 tsp salt
1/8 tsp garlic powder
1/8 tsp paprika
2 – 3 tbsp shredded fresh Parmesan cheese

Directions

1. Heat grill. Cut 14-inch-square sheet of heavy-duty foil. Place potatoes in center.

2. In a small bowl, combine oil, Italian seasoning, salt, garlic powder and paprika. Drizzle over potatoes and stir gently to coat.

3. Wrap securely to create a pouch using double-fold seals.

4. Place foil packet on grill over medium heat for 30-40 minutes or until potatoes are tender.

5. Remove packet from grill and open. Sprinkle with cheese. Return to grill and cook an additional 5 minutes or until cheese is melted.

Number of Servings: 4

Table of Equivalents

Dash = 2-4 drops

3 teaspoons = 1 tablespoons = 1/2 fluid ounce = 15 milliliters

4 tablespoons = 1/4 cup = 2 fluid ounces = 60 milliliters

16 tablespoons = 1 cup (1/2 pint) = 8 fluid ounces = 240 milliliters

2 cup = 1 pint = 16 fluid ounces = 480 milliliters

2 pints = 1 quart = 32 fluid ounces = 960 milliliters

4 quarts = 1 gallon = 128 fluid ounces = 3840 milliliters

2 tablespoons = 1 ounce = 1/8 cup = 30 grams

4 tablespoons = 2 ounces = 1/4 cup = 60 grams

16 tablespoons = 8 ounces = 1 cup = 240 grams

2 cups = 16 ounces = 1 pound = 480 grams

#####

Thank you from Grace!

To my sister Rain, my biggest fan and cheerleader, and who will eat whatever I cook and put in front of her. Thanks for being there no matter what.

To Emily the Baker, for being my phone-a-chef when I need one.

To my family, who has been so supportive in my culinary adventures and endeavors, without you, I wouldn't eat the way I do.

To Honorée, for seeing in me what I couldn't see in myself, for believing in me, and for giving me the kick in the butt I that I need! Thank you so much for this opportunity. I am eternally grateful.

Thank you from Honorée!

To the single moms who inspired me to get this done and quickly!

To my "inner circle." Thank you for reinforcing that I can do anything and encouraging me to keep going. I appreciate you!

To my wonderful husband – Every day you give me another ten reasons to love you. I love you more and more (and more).

To Dino Marino – Another stroke of your genius ~ thank you!

To Grace ~ Thanks for helping me to feel like I could write a cookbook – and cook! -- with your help and encouragement.

Who is Grace?

Grace Bascos is a Las Vegas-based food writer who not only loves to eat, but more importantly, loves to cook. Her writing has appeared in publications such as People, Vegas Magazine and Tasting Panel Magazine, and she has appeared on the Frommers Radio Travel Show as an expert on Vegas dining.

In college, she found herself cooking in the kitchen of one of the popular campus restaurants, where she honed her techniques and her love of cooking for others. Hungry roommates and friends ensured that she wasn't only cooking at the restaurant, but constantly at home as well. Grace's love for food has taken her on travels around the country and the world, and she's always willing to try something new. Yet while she's slurped noodles in Hong Kong and roasted goat beachside in the Philippines, you'll never find her happier than when she's tucking into a perfect grilled cheese sandwich.

Grace Bascos
(312) 208-3123
http://www.IeatIdrinkIwrite.com
GBascos@gmail.com

Who is Honorée?

AUTHOR. Honorée is the author of *The Successful Single Mom* book series, *The Successful Single Dad, Tall Order!* and the upcoming *Vision to* Reality and Game *On!* She has created the Single Mom Transformation Program (SMTP™), The STMA™ 100-Day Action Plan Coaching Program, as well as The Tall Order! Success System and The Referral-Only Business System self-study courses.

SUCCESSFUL SINGLE MOM. Honorée is the proud mom of Lexi who, for some reason, wants to eat every day so that's really the reason she wrote this cookbook.

FOUNDER OF THE SINGLE MOM REVOLUTION. She wants single moms to own their greatness ~ to think of themselves as super heroines who can have, do, be and create anything and everything their heart's desire (and she wants the world to see them that way, too). Join the Revolution at http://www.singlemomrevolution.com.

BLISSED OUT NEWLYWED. Who wouldn't be blessed out with the husband who says, "I'll pick up something or make it myself." Or loves whatever she makes. *Be sure to hold out for your true Mr. Wonderful ~ it IS worth the wait.

BUDDING COOK. She can make every recipe in this book and gets a little better in the kitchen every day. If she can, you definitely can!

SINGLE MOM BLOG. Her blog reaches thousands of single moms each week, providing tips, tools, strategies, ideas and recipes for making the most of yourself, your mommy-ness, and your life. Join in the fun: http://thesuccessfulsinglemom.blogspot.com.

Honorée Enterprises, Inc.
http://www.HonoreeCorder.com
http://TheSuccessfulSingleMom.blogspot.com
Honoree@HonoreeCorder.com
Twitter: http://twitter.com/Honoree
Facebook: http://facebook.com/Honoree

Made in the USA
Lexington, KY
26 November 2016